Rising Out The Pit Of Rejection

Dominique M. Johnson

Rising Out The Pit of Rejection

Dominique M. Johnson

All scripture quotations are taken from the Holy Bible, New King James Version (NKJV) and Amplified Bible (AMP)

ISBN

Printed in USA

Table of Contents

Dedication

I dedicate this book to every person who has struggled with rejection and their identity. I pray that through the struggles of my life, you may enter a place of healing, truly surrendering to God and become the best version of yourself. May God reveal Himself to you in a new way.

Thank you, heavenly Father, for every obstacle because it brought me closer to you.

Chapter One: Left Behind

"Why don't you look like your dad? You know that he's not your daddy."

As a little girl, I always felt different. I always felt like there was something missing. When I was five years old, the world around looked so bright and brilliant! Then, at other times, the world seemed like the worst place ever. In the times where I felt the happiest, everything made sense until one day while I was at school. A little girl said to me, "Why don't you look like your dad? You know that he's not your daddy." She continued on, saying, "Dominique doesn't know who her daddy is." I responded saying "Shut up and leave me alone."

In that very moment, that brilliant light was completely shattered into a million pieces. The world felt like the darkest pit at that moment. The little girl had noticed that I did not look like the man who picked me up several times a week. Until that point, I did not know any other man to be my father. This little girl's probing completely unraveled five years of my young life. From that point, I started looking at my dad and comparing myself to him—even to my aunts and uncles. Unfortunately, that one question would take me on a quest that eventually led me down a horribly destructive place over and over during my life.

The day that I found the courage to ask my parents the big question started out like any other summer day. I was riding my bike with pink and white tassels on the side rails, accentuated with a bell on the handle bars. As I rode up and down the street as I had done so many times before, a minivan pulled up slowly beside me. Then, I heard a male's voice speaking to me.

"Dominique, it's me, Eric. Come here; I'm your dad."

Frightened, I immediately pedaled as hard as I could back towards my house where my parents were sitting. The minivan sped so fast past my house, it was crazy. My parents took me into the house and sat me down for "the talk." As soon as my behind hit the chair, the big question bubbled out of my mouth.

"Why don't I look like my dad?" Their countenances were of complete sadness. No one said anything for a moment although it felt like an eternity.

"Well, Dominique, technically this is not your blood father," my mother finally responded. "He is your stepfather and the man that drove by is your blood father."

At that very moment, it finally made sense why the little girl from school asked me that question. As I sat there I felt like the whole world had lied to me my entire life. Ever since that day, I thought about the man in the van and wondered if he thought about me. I only remember seeing my biological father a few times during childhood.

From that point forward, my life was filled with so many ups and downs that I stopped keeping up with them all. Many times when my household was in an upswing, I was very happy especially because my parents were seemingly getting along with one another. Other times, I desperately wanted to run away, never to return because the arguing, fussing and fighting kept me up at night. I would lay in bed and pray to God, not even knowing if He heard me. I asked Him to rescue me and take me to a different place where it was quiet and peaceful. Even though my parents would argue, I always knew that they loved me unconditionally. However, at times it was so hard for me to feel.

My stepdad took me everywhere with him until I was about nine or ten years old when it abruptly ended. By that time, my little sister was a toddler, and it seemed like she was the shining child. My stepdad and my mother didn't say anything negatively to me, but it bothered me with how they looked at her and how my stepdad's family always received her openly.

I knew that my parents loved me; however, I still was missing something. I felt like I had a hole in my heart or a void of some sort. Although I had a beautiful little sister, we were different in so many ways. I would always question why my biological dad didn't want to come see about me. There were times I thought he was planning to surprise me and pick me up one day. Unfortunately, my dreams of my biological father coming to get me did not come to pass.

Some nights, I stayed up, staring at my bedroom ceiling and thinking that maybe it was something wrong with me. I felt like, if the person who helped bring me into the world didn't want anything to do with me then this situation was impossible. This left me with this great desire to be accepted that never seemed to be able to be filled with anything.

See, the enemy never considered that although he planted seeds of abandonment and rejection in my life, God already made a way of escape for me (1 Corinthians 10:13). Around the time when my very young class mate pointed out that I looked different than the man who picked me up from school, the Lord had already planned to reveal Himself to me.

I remember that day like it was yesterday. I was around five or six years old with my mom at Wings of Love Missionary Baptist Church, standing up during worship as I've done so many times before. However, this particular moment felt different. As I was standing next to my mother, while I was singing, I felt a warmth come over my entire body. Not knowing why I began to feel this way, my only response to this feeling was to lift my hands. In that moment, I began to cry uncontrollably. I reached up towards my mom and she bent down to my level.

"Dominique, what's the matter?"

"Mama, I don't know but God touched me, and I can't stop crying," I barely got the words out.

"That's the Holy Spirit!" My mom responded, she stood back up, turned around and continued to worship.

In that very moment as I stood there with my hands lifted, I heard the voice of God, our Eternal Father, for the first time in my life. I didn't know it then, but from that very moment my life would never be the same. I was completely overwhelmed with emotion and somewhere inside of me, I knew that this had to be good because I knew I was safe and important to someone. At five or six years of age with limited understanding, I knew that God was absolutely real. God Himself came for me so that I would not be fatherless and without identity.

A father of the fatherless and a judge and protector of the widows, Is God in His holy habitation. God makes a home for the lonely; He leads the prisoners into prosperity, Only the stubborn and rebellious dwell in a parched land. Psalm 68:5-6 AMP

Looking back on that time of my life, I can clearly see now that heaven had a plan for me. The enemy knew that rejection from a parent would be a hard block to move because it causes the child to question the motive behind the parent's choice. Ultimately, the child feels devalued and carry themselves in this manner potentially for the rest of their life. Some may say, "Well Dominique, at least you had a stepdad and mother who cared for you and loved you." My response would be, "Yes, my parents did love me and took care of me but because they experienced rejection as children themselves. It would be hard for them to speak over me and guide me towards purpose, if they never dealt with their own issues." The problem in most families is that if our parents are still broken from their experiences, never receive healing or discover their identity in Christ, then their children ultimately won't know who or who's they are either.

In Luke 15:3-7, Jesus tells the parable about the lost sheep. *"What man among you, if he has a hundred sheep and loses one of them, does not leave the ninety-nine in the wilderness and go after the one which is lost, [searching] until he finds it? And when he has found it, he lays it on his shoulders, rejoicing. And when he gets home, he calls together his friends and his neighbors, saying to them, 'Rejoice with me, because I have found my lost sheep!' I tell you, in the same way there will be more joy in heaven over one sinner who repents than over ninety-nine righteous people who have no need of repentance"* (Luke 15:4-7 AMP)

See, God knows all things. He knows the ways we will take, no matter how far we go on the road. The beautiful thing about our God is that He is a good father. He will leave the ninety-nine others to find you, save you, bring you home and joyfully rejoice over your return.

> *"In the same way, I tell you, there is joy in the presence of the angels of God over one sinner who repents [that is, changes his inner self—his old way of thinking, regrets past sins, lives his life in a way that proves repentance; and seeks God's purpose for his life]."* Luke 15:10 AMP

Although now I can look back over this time in my life and see the many blessings God had given me, many of which I just could not understand. By the time I was twenty-two, I began to face and dig through my issues with rejection. Sitting in my apartment, the Lord began to deal with me concerning *forgiveness.* Forgiveness is the vehicle that God uses to take us on the journey to healing. Unfortunately, many of us do not want to ride in that vehicle because we want to remain angry, bitter, victimized and hurt. For many of us, we just learn to bury all the past emotional hurts, only to face them again when life triggers these past experiences. If you never decide to face the past, ultimately the enemy wins because you become stagnant, emotionally dwarfed while never really experiencing true liberation.

Once the Lord explained to me that forgiveness is not really about the other person nor does it excuse the things that they did or didn't do, but that it actually frees me from the past, I was more willing to ride with Him. I had to make a choice between life and death. Was I going to allow the past rejection and abandonment of the father who chose not to be a part of my life rule my life, or would I forgive him? I decided, from my heart and soul, to forgive the father who was never present. I forgave him for all the missed birthdays, missed events, missed games, missed graduations and even the few missed promises. I made a choice to grow and become a healthier, whole person.

As I close this chapter, I challenge you to think about the people from your past who abandoned, rejected, ignored, and hurt you. I want you to choose *in your heart* to forgive them—not because what they did, *did not* impact you, but so they can no longer dominate you emotionally. If you do not forgive, then they will have power over you and your emotional well-being forever. No one should have that type of power over your emotions except the Creator of the universe.

For if you forgive others their trespasses [their reckless and willful sins], your heavenly Father will also forgive you. But if you do not forgive others [nurturing your hurt and anger with the result that it interferes with your relationship with God], then your Father will not forgive your trespasses.

Matthew 6:14-15 AMP

Let all bitterness and wrath and anger and clamor [perpetual animosity, resentment, strife, fault-finding] and slander be put away from you, along with every kind of malice [all spitefulness, verbal abuse, malevolence]. Be kind and helpful to one another, tender-hearted [compassionate, understanding], forgiving one another [readily and freely], just as God in Christ also forgave you.

Ephesians 4:31-32 AMP

Pray this prayer:

Heavenly Father, I come before you a broken soul. I desire your peace and the safety of feeling your love for me. I desire to be made whole in every way. I ask that you come into my heart and take all the hurt, sadness, grief,

loss and emotions tied to every person or situation that left me dismayed. I ask that you replace those things with your love, your desire and most importantly, your Spirit. Your Word says that you will never leave me or forsake me, so rush into my life and my heart. Teach me how to forgive your way and display your character more daily.
In Jesus' name. Amen.

Chapter Two: The Trauma

Oftentimes, we'll experience what most people would classify as "normal" family trials. But what if I told you that many of our childhood and/or adolescent experiences were not "normal," but *traumatic*? Some people would agree; however, some would respond by saying, "Things happen" and "Learn to move on past it."

So, here is the problem with the thought process of "just move on with life." Sometimes, people will tell you to learn how to move on; however, the reality is that we are simply learning to keep secrets, suppress the hurt, dig wells of rejection and abandonment which creates cycles of dysfunction along with a host of other forms of destructive thinking.

As discussed in chapter one, my biological father was not in my life while I was growing up. This created a longing in me to know him even though he was not around. Because of his absence, seeds of rejection and abandonment took root in my young soul.

I literally felt like a lost child. Although my family always told me that I was beautiful, and affirmed my gifts and talents, deep down inside, I didn't believe them. When I looked at myself in the mirror, I did not see what my family saw when they looked at me. Because I didn't realize my worth, this opened a door for the enemy to come in and distort my way of thinking.

Please know that the enemy will take full advantage of you in any way he can. Because of the trauma of not knowing where I came from, my self-worth plummeted dramatically. There were times when I smiled for family pictures and yet, I secretly hated myself for not being enough for a parent who I did not even know.

Allow me to take a moment to point out another trick of the enemy. See, hell desires to introduce destructive cycles early on in our lives. The cycle of self-trauma from the enemy caused me to display a beautiful smile although inwardly I was crushed. I am so sure that you can empathize with this feeling if you've ever experienced any level of rejection in your life.

In our family culture, sometimes we are raised to carry burdens and secrets that ultimately causes stagnation our own lives. We are raised to believe that if we even think that we want to talk about our trauma, we are viewed as "weak."

Please know that you are not weak for wanting to discuss your feelings about the trauma you've experienced.

We must stop declaring and equating dysfunction with normality. We must learn to speak the truth and implement change so that our daughters and sons will never feel like they are silently drowning in their own sorrow and trauma. Be the first in your family to kill this horrible mindset that seeks to continually destroy lives daily.

Maybe you were hurt, dropped, and abandoned; but I want to remind you that Jesus was there the whole time. I can only tell you this because He was there during every moment of trauma I experienced. Despite the enemy's relentless attempts to attack and beat me down emotionally and mentally as a young child, God never left my side.

Despite my young age, I knew God was real. At times when I would be coloring or playing, I heard a still small voice say to me, "I'm still here. You're special to me." I never really told anyone that I was hearing a voice talk to me because sometimes, that was the only voice that brought me comfort, feelings of inner safety and peace. While hell's plan for me was playing out daily, so was heaven's plan. The Father of the universe always stayed no matter what happened or what was on the horizon.

Where can I go from Your Spirit? Or where can I flee from Your presence? If I ascend to heaven, You are there; If I make my bed in Sheol (the nether world, the place of the dead), behold, You are there. If I take the wings of the dawn, If I dwell in the remotest part of the sea, Even there Your hand will lead me, And Your right hand will take hold of me.

Psalm 139:7-10 AMP

As I got older, the brilliant light that I described in chapter one returned. I thought less about the father who was not there and started enjoying just being a kid. I began to enjoy playing with my sibling and even made some childhood friends. Eventually, I found myself laughing more and enjoying some alone time while playing with my dolls. If I only knew that all the fun would end just as fast as it began.

Have you ever experienced anything that seemed to be normal before the worst storm of your life hit? Well, I would have never imagined that I would experience a tornado at eight years old. I started a new school at this age, and it was supposed to be a good thing since the school was closer to other family. At the time, my mom was working a lot and it was more convenient for me to attend school near family and walk to school with family.

At the time, I thought it would be so cool to be able to hang out with my older cousins. As the younger cousin, I did not really hang out with them often. Every day, my mom would drop me off over my family member's house and I would wait to walk to school in the mornings. I thought it was cool to walk to school with my cousins because other kids in school who had older sibling(s) would walk along with us. This was my opportunity to make new friends especially since I was in a new school.

Over the course of the school year, rapid changes took place. My cousin suddenly became very playful and silly with me—more than ever before. After our walk home from school, when we got back to his house, he started doing things like coming out the bathroom with his pants down and would make jokes about that. These scenarios happened more often and they quickly advanced.

One day after school, I sat on the couch in the basement watching television. My cousin came and stood before me without pants or underwear. Immediately I turned away and attempted to move off the couch, which was unsuccessful. In that very moment, I lost my innocence. I was forced to perform fellatio until I threw up. This horrible situation turned into a normal event for an eight-year-old little girl. I cried and begged him to not make me commit this horrible act, all to no avail. He became extremely aggressive with me at times to ensure that I feared him enough that I would not tell.

Day after day, I felt dirty, sad, ashamed and scared as he started fondling me more often. I would go home and look at my mom with a desire to tell her to never to send me back there. Then I thought about all the times my cousin said,

"If you ever tell, no one is going to believe you anyway."

This very statement ran through my mind every time I had to endure these horrid acts. My personality progressively faded away with each traumatic experience. The fun-loving, silly little girl that I had always been no longer existed. I evolved into a girl who didn't like to look at herself in the mirror and no longer stood up for herself. I evolved into a girl who cried in the shower and felt smaller than an ant most times. Even as I secretly endured all this trauma, the Lord always seemed to have a ram in the bush. The Lord always made sure that He kept Himself in my view no matter the situation and provided ways of escape for my young soul.

When they came to the place of which God had told him, Abraham built an altar there and arranged the wood, and bound Isaac his son and placed him on the altar, on top of the wood. Abraham reached out his hand and took the knife to kill his son. But the Angel of the LORD called to him from heaven and said, "Abraham, Abraham!"

He answered, "Here I am." The LORD said, "Do not reach out [with the knife in] your hand against the boy, and do nothing to [harm] him; for now I know that you fear God

[with reverence and profound respect], since you have not withheld from Me your son, your only son [of promise]." Then Abraham looked up and glanced around, and behold, behind him was a ram caught in a thicket by his horns. And Abraham went and took the ram and offered it up for a burnt offering (ascending sacrifice) instead of his son.

Genesis 22:9-13 AMP

In the midst of horrible school days and enduring tremendous distress, the Lord was always there with me. During this time, my mother was working a lot of hours all the time and she needed someone to be with me and my sibling in the evening and weekends. One day, my mother told me that I would have a new babysitter. My first thought was relief until I panicked on the inside in fear of leaving one horrid situation to go right into another.

"Hey, come take a walk with me," my mother said to me. Excited to be with my mom, I immediately ran to her side and we began walking down the street. We only had walked about nine houses down the street before my mom started walking up a driveway. *Why are we here?* I thought to myself. It was not until I saw this short African American woman walking out her side door and through her gate that I knew something was up. I saw this woman smiling at my mother before turning her smile in my direction. As we got closer to this woman, my mother turned to me and spoke.

"Dominique, this is Ms. Lloyd. Say hello." So of course I spoke to her and she responded saying, "Good afternoon, beautiful." My mother and Ms. Lloyd stood by the gate and talked and laughed for quite a while. Before we left, Ms. Lloyd prayed with my mother. I had not seen anything like this before except at church, so I thought it was strange. As we walked back home, my mother said, "that's your new babysitter."

I was completely scared the first time I went to Ms. Lloyd's house. I wondered how this woman was going to be with me and my little sister. When we entered into her home, she was very nice and pleasant. She immediately took us to the basement, which I thought was strange until I got down there. It was like a whole house in the basement. She had it set up with a living room area and toys. There was a set of doors that opened to an entire kitchen area. I was shocked, but the even bigger shocker was that *I felt safe there*.

Over the next few months, I found myself loving being down there at her house. In fact, I loved being at her house so much that I would forget how horrible it was being with my older cousin on school days. Ms. Lloyd was a Bible believing, Holy Ghost-filled woman who prayed aloud often, filling my young ears with words I could not understand. Oftentimes, she made me pray with her. She kept her television tuned to TBN most of the day. These shows on TBN were filled with preachers declaring the word of the Lord. She taught me the books of the Bible, had me to read Scriptures and then explain to her what God was saying. At the time, I did not understand why she did this, but I understood later in life.

Ms. Lloyd taught me the power of prayer and holiness before the Lord. She would pray for me often. She knew me so well; she could discern when I was not myself especially after I came there after leaving my cousin's house. One day, I came into the basement and she looked at me and said, "Dominique, don't you know that the Lord hears you when you talk to Him? God will answer you if you tell Him and He will fix it." I could not even respond; I just stood there and cried. Ms. Lloyd immediately hugged me and began to pray. From that very moment, God showed me that He saw me and my situation.

Ms. Lloyd continued to be our babysitter for almost a year and a half. Even though she knew that my young soul was carrying a burden, she never pressured me to tell, and I was too afraid to tell her the truth. As time went by, I kept this horrible secret from every person who was able to help me because I feared that no one would believe me.

One day, I walked down the street to visit Ms. Lloyd and play in her yard.

I knocked on the door for few minutes and there was no

answer. So I went back home and told my mother. My mother immediately began to make phone calls to find out where she was. Several hours later, we found out that Ms. Lloyd was in the hospital and she was very sick. My mother found out that Ms. Lloyd had been hiding her cancer diagnosis from everyone and she had refused treatment.

Even as a young girl, I knew that her sickness had to be serious because when Ms. Lloyd returned home, she was not herself. She stayed in bed most of the time or on the couch, which I never saw in the time that I had known her. I would go down the street and try to help her eat more or whatever I could. Ms. Lloyd always tried to muster up energy to sit up with me. She sang old hymns and read the Bible to me. She told me about God's love for me and how He was a healer and how He was always on time.

One day, I went to visit her like I had done so many times before, but this time was different. I sat in the bed with her with the Bible open. She spoke very softly to me this particular day. She talked to me about forgiveness and that I should never walk away from God. She read so many Scriptures over me and then she prayed very fervently over me.

"Dominique, God is always going to be with you, no matter what. Pray always and love God with all your heart, soul and mind."

"Yes, I always will," I responded. This was our last conversation. A few days later, she passed away.

Jesus answered, "The first and most important one is: 'HEAR, O ISRAEL, THE LORD OUR GOD IS ONE LORD; AND YOU SHALL LOVE THE LORD YOUR GOD WITH ALL YOUR HEART, AND WITH ALL YOUR SOUL (life), AND WITH ALL YOUR MIND (thought, understanding), AND WITH ALL YOUR STRENGTH.'"

Mark 12:29-30 AMP

The day that my mom told me that Ms. Lloyd had passed away, I felt so lost even though I knew in my heart that she was sick. I felt like one of my safe places was stolen away from me, along with the person who brought so much joy into my life. I knew that I would have to continue going through trauma with no place of real peace. I am so sure that you can relate to this feeling of great loss. It feels like your heart will be broken forever. Even though I had only known her for a short timeframe, my then nine-year-old self was even more confused about how this so-called good life would turn out for me. I continued to endure molestation for a little while longer before God created an exit for me.

Sometime after Ms. Lloyd transitioned, my mom told me and my sister that we were going to be moving and

I immediately was excited. I knew that this would be a great thing for me. Before we were able to move, my cousin found out and made those last few weeks a living hell for me. He made me watch porn tapes with him that were hidden in my aunt's room. While we watched the tapes, he told me that he was going to make me do the things in the videos. He touched all over my body reenacting what he saw in the videos. Meanwhile, I cried and begged him not to touch me. Eventually I stopped crying and would just let him do it because the tears never stopped him anyway. I was broken at this point.

The last day that I was there alone with him, things appeared as if it was going to be another day of the same old crap. Sitting in the basement on the couch, my heart skipped a beat when I heard a car door close. Then I heard the jingle of keys and the back door open. I was so happy to see my aunt walk through that back door that I ran to the bottom of the basement stairs and made sure my aunt saw and spoke to me.

She kicked off her nursing shoes and headed to the bathroom to shower, but I knew that I was safe from the usual. A little while later, my mom called the house phone and said she was on her way to pick me up. I quickly got all my things together so that I was ready when she pulled up. The moment I heard the horn blow, I rushed up the stairs, said bye to my aunt and walked out knowing that I would not have to see this house or my cousin for a very long time. Riding away in the car with my mom was the most peace I had in over a year, and I was glad to have it.

Chapter Three: Rooted In

Peace is defined as a normal, non-warring condition of a nation, group of nation or the world. I found myself in this place called peace and it seemed as if the everything had come to a steady, consistent and normal place. At this time, we had moved to the other side of town and we had been there for almost a year or so. I was about to turn 10 years old and for a time, I had forgotten about those traumatic experiences. I felt carefree as if somehow God had actually heard my cries and rewarded me with this place of peace. Just when I thought that everything had made a swing for the better, I was wrong.

It was beautiful summer day, and my step dad was about to go over his friend's house. I asked to go along with him because other kids would always be there, and I always had fun with them. The day was going great. I had a ball playing with the other kids while we rode bikes and played freeze tag.

Just like any other kid, when I heard the ice cream truck, of course I wanted a cone. I began to look for my dad to ask for some money to buy my ice cream. I looked around outside for him in his friend's yard and he was nowhere to be found. I asked my dad's friend if he saw him, and he told me that my dad had to be in the house. So, I went to look for him.

When I got into the house, I started calling for him and did not get any response initially. I looked in the direction of the bathroom only to see the door was closed. When I looked to my left, I saw another closed door; however, I heard my dad's voice coming from behind that door. I knocked and opened the door at the same time.

"Daddy, I was looking…" the words to my sentence seemed to vanish upon seeing my dad having sex with a woman I had never seen before.

"Close the door!" he yelled at me. And I quickly closed the door, ran outside and sat on the front porch step, confused at what I just saw. My dad's friend came up to me and said, "Did you find your dad? Here is some money, baby girl. Get your ice cream before the truck leaves." Dazed and confused, I never responded to his question. I got up, bought my ice cream and returned to porch step. I had absolutely no understanding as to what I had just seen. My dad eventually came out of the house. I was still sitting on that step as he walked right past me. He never said a word to me about anything.

When I returned home with my dad, I went into the house and went straight to my room. I did not know what I should do with what I saw. When my mom got home, of course she asked me if I had a great time playing.

“Yeah, it was cool,” I responded. My mom immediately knew something was not right, so she began to ask other questions. After about the third question, I began to cry and told my mom what I had witnessed. She hugged me and explained that it was going to be alright. However, I knew within me that it was not going to be okay.

Once my mom got herself together, she confronted my dad and of course, it turned into a huge argument. My dad called me liar and said that I made up the whole thing. Although my parents were in the basement, you can only imagine how loud they were screaming back and forth at one another. When my young ears heard my dad tell my mother that I lied to her, my heart was yet again broken by a man who was supposed to be an honest fatherly example. At that very moment, I knew that my relationship with him would never be the same.

As time went by, I always felt that my dad no longer liked me because he always seemed angry with me. It seemed like I couldn’t do anything right in his eyes. From that moment, my parent’s arguments escalated to another level. There were days that they screamed at one another until the early mornings several times a week. To make things worse, they would drink alcohol. It got to a place that one day, I went to where they were arguing and yelled, *“Shut up! We can’t sleep ever!”*

"Oh, I'm sorry. Go back to bed," my mom apologized. See, what my parents did not understand or choose to see was that they were causing more damage than good. Dysfunction and trauma seek to kill your soul and make you believe that it should be your norm. Now I know why it's so important for us to not just be around the things of God, but to have a real relationship with Him that shows us ourselves to change so we don't cause more trauma.

Fathers, do not provoke or irritate or exasperate your children [with demands that are trivial or unreasonable or humiliating or abusive; nor by favoritism or indifference; treat them tenderly with lovingkindness], so they will not lose heart and become discouraged or unmotivated [with their spirits broken].
Colossians 3:21 AMP

Things got worse over time. My parents' arguments continued, as well as the drinking. By this time, I was so over all of it and just wanted to return to the time of peace which seemed so far behind me. I became the kid who yelled at their parents to stop arguing. I begged them to chill so we—the kids—would not have to suffer. My attitude was so horrible, and I found myself always angry with my parents. My life in my own definition was horrible. I just knew that my future was going to be that same way.

Many times, I thought that something must really be wrong with me because I always felt that I messed things up in some way. I thought to myself, *Dang, Dominique. How did you mess up with both your dads and end up miserable every day?* As days turned into months, I tried my best to keep a low profile. I would either be in my room or outside playing to stay out of my parents' way. I did my best to do all of my chores so my parents would not be upset with me. This became the new way I chose to handle my stress and dysfunction. Overall, my life seemed to be working. I became so good at staying out of the way, I would often spend nights and weekends at my cousin's house just to get away and play. By the time I turned eleven, my life went from bad to worse.

I remember that day just like it was yesterday, along with the absolute hurt, pain and heaviness that accentuated the day. I went to school like any other day, and everything seemed normal until I was called to the office over the PA system. When I entered the office, I saw my mother sitting in the chair waiting for me.

"Is everyone okay? Why am I in the office?" I asked my mom.

"We have some things to do, so go get your things," my mom responded. I immediately went to my locker and left with my mother. I thought it was quite strange. We rode in complete silence—no music, no singing like normal from my mom—it was completely silent. We pulled up in the driveway of our house, and I got out the car like usual. I went in the house and changed my clothes. As I walked towards the entrance of the living room, I wasn't prepared for the conversation that was about to happen.

"Dominique, I want you to be honest with me," my mom said. "Has anybody ever touched you or made you touch them?" I did not respond immediately, but as soon as I opened my mouth to respond, I started crying uncontrollably. In that moment, I felt like the weight of this secret that had been crushing me so long was finally lifting.

I told my mother all of the things that had happened to me during that timeframe with my older cousin, and my mother held me and cried with me. I remember asking my mom why she decided to ask me this on that day.

"The Lord told me in my dreams."

I was absolutely floored by that response. In my heart, it reassured me that the Lord knew me because He made sure I would not carry this horrible secret with me for the rest of my life.

For there is nothing hidden that will not become evident, nor anything secret that will not be known and come out into the open.

Luke 8:17 AMP

At this very moment while your eyes are upon this page, I want to release something to you. God has seen all of your trauma, loss, abuse, neglect and every other horrible place in your life. But know that you have a person who lives to make intercession (pray) for you. God never leaves us to be taken advantage of forever. He is a true father who makes sure to let us know that He sees everything and will always protect us. You are probably thinking how did He protect you? The mere fact that the Lord would allow my mother to not only dream but retain the memory to speak to me lets me know that God's intentions was for me to move past this without feeling the sting of the trauma. God always takes care of us even when we do not understand why we had to endure the evil that the enemy brings into our lives.

"I have told you these things, so that in Me you may have [perfect] peace. In the world you have tribulation and distress and suffering, but be courageous [be confident, be undaunted, be filled with joy]; I have overcome the world." [My conquest is accomplished, My victory abiding.]"

John 16:33 AMP

Therefore He is able also to save forever (completely, perfectly, for eternity) those who come to God through Him, since He always lives to intercede and intervene on their behalf [with God].

Hebrews 7:25 AMP

The weeks following this moment of confession were filled with lots of discussion with my mother. My mother eventually told me that I would have to face my cousin who did these horrible things to me. I was completely against this because I was scared. I did not want everyone to know because I would feel dirty all over again verbalizing the things he did to me.

The day I went with my mother to a local park to meet up with my cousin and his mother was one the scariest days of my life at that time. My hands were completely sweaty as I walked up to them. Standing by my mother as she spoke with my cousin's mother, I knew this was going to go bad. As my mother explained the reason for the meeting, my cousin stared at me as if he wanted to kill me on sight.

My mother had me to explain to his mother, what her son had done to me all those days I spent at her house. Of course, my cousin lied and denied it all; however, I was completely shocked by his mother's response. She stood in front of me and my mother and said that I made it up to cover up that I was letting a boy feel me up and do inappropriate things to me. She called me a whore and said that no one would believe me anyway. She also said that she would make sure that all my family knew I was a whore so they would never speak to me again. I knew that the very words my cousin's mother spoke were going to be her mission for this situation.

Not long after this meeting, many of my aunts let it be known that I was not welcomed at their homes. It was known throughout my family circle that I was the one who accused my older cousin of horrible things. All the relationships I had with my other female cousins disappeared so very quickly. I felt completely alone. I felt like I lost twice once experiencing the abuse and secondly by my family's rejection because no one believed me except my own mother.

Memories of this day would forever be replayed many times in my mind. After this unfortunate meeting ended, we never spoke about the situation or the outcome. At this young age, I had to experience the humiliation of going to the "female doctor" to make sure that everything down below was still intact and normal.

Here's a revelation I got concerning the enemy. The enemy does not care how much he will expose your weakness, traumas, pain, or family turmoil. The goal is to leave you in a perpetual place of humiliation, pain, trauma and secrecy to keep you bound so you'll never experience true freedom. Although the enemy was quite successful in his tactics, he still is no match against his own creator. God always will be many steps ahead of the enemy's plan.

Although you may have gone through something similar, God will use the same pain, trauma, humiliation as a weapon against the one that sent the destruction. Jesus made an open show of the enemy and used what the enemy had considered weak, which was his flesh and humanity to completely embarrass him. It was that same flesh and blood that brought us back into alignment with our Heavenly Father and destroyed the enemies plans.

When He had disarmed the rulers and authorities [those supernatural forces of evil operating against us], He made a public example of them [exhibiting them as captives in His triumphal procession], having triumphed over them through the cross.
Colossians 2:15 AMP

So many times, our situations create opportunities for isolation that some of us never seem to break free from in our lifetime. I became the epitome of isolation.
I did not have many friends at this time in my life. I learned

to stay to myself most times which only reinforced the emotions that I felt. I felt as if no one else in the world felt as bad as I did during these moments. Understand that isolation, fear, trauma and pain will plague your mind, constantly making you feel as if you're the reason for it all.

I will never forget the moments where the enemy played with my mind, causing me to think life would be better if I weren't living in it. I had these terrible horrific nightmares where I died repeatedly. These nightmares occurred so frequently that I believed it was a sign or something.

I remember this day so vividly. I was twelve years old and was on summer vacation. I had survived a school year filled with ups and down, bullying by multiple girls, fighting parents and loneliness to no end. It was a warm summer day and my parents had been arguing the night before. As usual, I tried to stop them for the millionth time but was unsuccessful. That very next morning, I got yelled at because I forgot to complete a task my mother had asked me to do. I remember her saying to me, "Why don't you get it? I am so sick and tired of talking to you, saying the same things over again."

In that moment, I completed the task she asked of me and she left to run errands. My thoughts were centered around how not useful I was, and how tired everyone was of me. I thought about how horrible I had to be for my own mother to be sick and tired of me. I made up my mind: I was done and was going commit suicide. I was going to slit my wrist and bleed out on my mother's couch.

I went into the kitchen and got sharpest knife I could find. I went into the living room totally prepared to take my own life with no thought about anything else except being out of the pain and torment I felt. Holding the knife in my right hand, I took the sharpest part of the knife and placed it on my left wrist. As I pressed the knife into my skin and saw the skin break, I heard the loudest voice speak to me.

"No!" At that moment, I dropped the knife on the floor and watched the drips of blood flow from my wrist. Everything in me knew that God, the Father of all creation opened heaven wide enough so that I could clearly hear Him speak and stop me from ending the life He gave me. Moments later, my mother pulled back into our driveway and blew the horn for me to come and help with bringing in the groceries. So, I quickly picked up the knife, cleaned my mess, stuck a band-aid on my wrist and ran outside. My mother, of course, noticed the band-aid very quickly and I replied with a believable lie unfortunately. From that day until this day, I never attempted to take my life again because deep down, I knew God had more for me than those moments.

Please understand that the enemy studies you and your blood line. The whole agenda is to keep you repeating the same situations and scenarios of those who came before you. See, at that time in my life, I did not know that my own mother experienced the same type of trauma that I had experienced. My mother's father was absent in her life and she was abused as well growing up. God always has a way of stopping the foolishness, but person He chooses must choose Him back.

The Bible speaks about no man being able to come to Christ unless He draws you to Himself. The enemies that were attempting to overtake me had no clue that I would be the one who would one to boldly stand and declare that the buck stops here. I challenge you today to purpose in your heart to surrender fear, intimidation, shame, guilt, hurt and disappointment from people and situations to God. He is truly the only one who can carry the weight of all these emotions and pain. The enemy loves to live and thrive in the secret place in our hearts and minds because secrets produce shame which keeps you bound. Pray this prayer and choose to release it all at the feet of Jesus.

Heavenly Father, I thank you for this day that you have made. I humbly come before you, nakedly exposing my heart before you. Lord, I ask that you heal every old, open wound of my past that was caused by the decisions of others. Lord, remove the guilt, shame, secrets, lies of the enemy and the spirits that replay old situations. Remove the fear and embarrassment of these evil and vile places from my past.

Lord, I desire to be made whole in my emotions, in my mind and mindset, my decisions, how I treat people and most importantly, in my soul and spirit. Today I choose to forgive every person who've caused me to feel these things. I release them from my heart. Fill those places with your love and peace. Heal me and heal the broken pieces of them so they can truly know you. Thank you, Father God, that from this moment forward, I will never be that old broken person.

I am made whole in Christ Jesus right now. Amen.

"No one can come to Me unless the Father who sent Me draws him [giving him the desire to come to Me]; and I will raise him up [from the dead] on the last day. It is written in the prophets, 'AND THEY WILL ALL BE TAUGHT OF GOD.' Everyone who has listened to and learned from the Father,

comes to Me."

John 6:44-45 AMP

"Come to Me, all who are weary and heavily burdened [by religious rituals that provide no peace], and I will give you rest [refreshing your souls with salvation]. Take My yoke upon you and learn from Me [following Me as My disciple], for I am gentle and humble in heart, and YOU WILL FIND REST (renewal, blessed quiet) FOR YOUR SOULS.

For My yoke is easy [to bear] and My burden is light."

Matthew 11:28-30 AMP

Chapter Four: Decisions

Life is a series of daily choices. We do not consider the consequences of such decisions at that moment upon making them. I'm here to let you know that every choice can have either a positive effect or negative effect. Before we understand the importance of making proper choices, we tend to do whatever we feel is convenient at the time. So, in many of our cases, the trauma we've experienced was the combination of choices made by others who had no idea of the consequences those choices would create. My cousin's decision that traumatized me was not my choice, or the fact that I grew up in a home filled with constant conflict and strife. But all their choices effected the way that I would make decisions for so many years later.

One would imagine that things should have gotten a bit better, especially considering that all the dirt was out in the open. As I continued to blossom into my teenage years, many of the same hurdles I faced showed up again. Around age thirteen, my biological father showed back up in my life, making all sort of promises and apologizing for all the time that he had missed. Still feeling rejected and abandoned by him, I excitedly believed it all. I figured why would he come to find me if he did not want to spend time with me or get to know me? Well, sorry to say, but as you can guess he did not stay around or keep his promises. He found ways to make me feel less than because I didn't call him all the time and according to him, I wasn't trying to have a relationship with him.

Let me insert this notion to you. Many of our issues with insecurity and lack of self-worth come from the very people who should affirm us. I know now that this portion of my life introduced me to a spirit of people pleasing. Pleasing others made me feel that in order for me to be accepted by others, I needed to make sure I always did everything to make sure others would always be good with me. I tried calling my biological father more often, leaving message after message only to get half conversations, more lies and a bigger hole in my heart. Having that level of hurt pushed me to a place that I despised the idea of *any man*, father or not.

One time as a young teen, I completely hated the idea of liking boys. I wore baggy basketball shorts, big shirts and always wore my hair in a ponytail. I hated when my mother would make me dress up. There was a time when the enemy attempted to sway me towards liking girls. I remembered thinking that it would be so much easier that way because all boys do is hurt you, embarrass you, and lie to you; so what is the point? Although I battled my nature, I still somehow felt connected to God. Around this same time, I began to read my Bible, not really understanding a lot of the message but for some reason, I always found something to relate to.

I want you to notice a theme here. Many times, as the enemy attempted to bring deception into my life and your life, God always found a way to get something to me and you. I want you to remember that God is always speaking to us in our time of need and distress; however, we often do not recognize it because He speaks in the still small voice. Many times, God is trying to call us out of dark places and our caves, but we are expecting Him to move so mightily that we miss Him.

So He said, "Go out and stand on the mountain before the LORD." And behold, the LORD was passing by, and a great and powerful wind was tearing out the mountains and breaking the rocks in pieces before the LORD; but the LORD was not in the wind. And after the wind, [there was] an earthquake, but the LORD was not in the earthquake. After the earthquake, [there was] a fire, but the LORD was not in the fire; and after the fire, [there was] the sound of a gentle blowing. When Elijah heard the sound, he wrapped his face in his mantle (cloak) and went out and

stood in the entrance of the cave. And behold, a voice came to him and said, "What are you doing here, Elijah?"
1 Kings 19:11-13 AMP

Not much time after these thoughts and images flooded my mind, one my favorite aunts took me to church with her along with her older son. The service was typical until one lady began to pray over the mic. As she began to pray, she asked that everyone kneel right where they were at the moment. I found myself kneeling and I began to cry uncontrollably as if my heart was broken, because in reality it was. As I cried and prayed, I asked the Lord to come into my heart and change my life because up until that very moment, I felt that it sucked, and I had gotten the short end of every stick. I felt like He was the only one who understood me, knew me and saw me.

While I was kneeling on the floor of this church, I felt something shift in my heart. I couldn't tell you exactly what took place, but I know something moved and something changed. I felt moments of overwhelming grief, but then I felt wave after wave of what I can only describe as pure love. These waves rushed over me and calmed the pain and deep hurt. It felt like peace, contentment, and joy in my heart somehow.

Those moments on that floor, kneeling before God, became the tools I'd used to carry me through many of my early battles. Just as much as this moment would be a major brick in my foundation of my relationship with God, it was also a notice for all of hell. Darkness is able to set up situations to produce more evil in your life; however, God's ability to create moments for you to see, hear and feel Him allow you to have that split second to receive Him. Although darkness cannot do anything about you choosing God, the enemy can try its very best to make you change your mind, and unfortunately those tactics are successful.

After my encounter with the Lord, I developed a new outlook on life. I started thinking that I could have a life that didn't reflect the trauma I experienced. I attempted more often to read my Bible and understand God. As I began to do these things, other areas of my life continued to be uneasy.

My relationship with my mother and step-dad continued to be a struggle. I didn't even like my stepfather to speak to me sometimes. He would be so harsh that I don't even believe he recognized it. Often, my parents would blame the tension between us on me being a teenager or hormones. But the reality of the situation was that I did not feel emotionally safe to be there alone.

I started doing what typical teenagers would normally do. I talked on the phone to my few friends and to some extent, I became a bit rebellious. I found myself in a space that I did not really care what my parents were talking about because they didn't see me. I began to make choices that I thought would fill the holes I felt in my own soul. I began choosing people in my circle who were the opposite of who and what I stood for as a young lady. My friends at that time were doing all sorts of things like having sex, skipping schools, talking to multiple boys at the same time and all sorts of other foolish things. Although, I gave my life to Christ, I was still just a kid with no full understanding of the magnitude of my decision.

With that being said, I continued to do what any other teenage girl would do.

I attempted to fill the voids with boys. I talked to boys and snuck around like so many of us did at that age, but I took it up several notches. At age fourteen, I was talking to a young man who was 20 years old. We had met at a music camp I attended. I had conversations with this individual for long periods of time when I was home alone. Sometimes, I would sneak while my parents were home. This guy told me everything that a broken girl like myself wanted to hear. He told me how beautiful and smart I was, and how he thought my body was the most beautiful thing he had ever seen.

Because of the place I was in, I believed every word. He would meet me at my high school so we could see one another. We would embrace each other with a kiss, but I never let him go all the way. Somewhere in my mind, I knew that he was not the one I should give my body to.

Somehow, my mother found out about the young man. She nearly beat the black off my behind and threatened to report him to the police. I was crushed that the one boy who liked me was out of the picture permanently. I was so upset because I felt like I couldn't even talk to a guy without my mother finding out and me being embarrassed. Seemed like I would never feel love from the opposite sex ever. The seeds of rejection were growing and sprouting up vividly at this point in my life.

My deep longing to be wanted by the opposite sex and be accepted dominated my thoughts daily. The darkness of rejection and abandonment took over my life so much that I began to wallow in that place not ever believing that the light would come. In the Bible, Jesus spoke a profound statement about our sight and how it truly works. I did not see myself the way God saw me, and as a result, I had a skewed view of reality and ultimately myself. I made choices that would impact my life for many years to come.

"The eye is the lamp of the body; so if your eye is clear [spiritually perceptive], your whole body will be full of light [benefiting from God's precepts]. But if your eye is bad [spiritually blind], your whole body will be full of darkness [devoid of God's precepts]. So if the [very] light inside you [your inner self, your heart, your conscience] is darkness, how great and terrible is that darkness!
Matthew 6:22-23 AMP

The kingdom of darkness does not care who or what it has to use to take you out of alignment, purpose and identity; but I declare to you that life does not end at your point of bad decisions or mistakes. Your life will truly begin the moment you choose to never again make decisions out of your brokenness and rejection.

So after being restricted from communicating with this young (yet older) man, I sought out boys my age. I no longer put up fights when they wanted to touch my booty or when they tried to kiss me. To me, some attention was better than no attention at all. One day, I was playing basketball in the street with the neighborhood kids when a young teenage guy pulled up in his car and hopped out. He wanted to play as well. Because everyone was playing on my basketball rim, I demanded to know who he was and why he thought he could come and demand privileges. I found out quickly that he knew one of the other boys who were playing as well. Apparently, he had seen me multiple times playing and wanted my number. Although I was not feeling him like that, ultimately I gave him my number late that week.

During that time, we talked to each other often on the telephone. I was up late at night having conversations with this young man. We discussed our families and how we were raised. Often, we exchanged stories about our pain points and the rejection and abuse we both experienced. Our pain and rejection became the glue of our budding friendship. We told each other that we should be friends to protect one another from the pain of this crazy world and that somehow, we could overcome it together. I was fifteen and he was sixteen. We thought our individual brokenness was enough to repair each other's pain and make one another whole. Our high school love grew strong quickly. I went from being completely uninterested in boys to thinking about this guy.

I started sneaking out of the house to see him. I would literally climb out my window to sneak out to his house. I thought this was the coolest idea yet because I would wait until my parents were asleep so no one would miss me. I would return before they would awake early the next morning. I loved being with this guy. He made me feel special and he focused on me all the time. He wrote songs for me; we listened to old school music and dreamed of this happy life we would create. I quickly fell for him, believing that I was all he ever wanted in his life. I was determined to prove to him that I was not like other girls who would reject him. I would love him and show him how much he meant to me—so much so that I decided to lose my virginity to him.

One summer evening, I snuck out the house and went to his home. I thought that if I had sex with him, it would prove my love. I thought he would always be there, and he would never hurt me. In the moments before I had sex, I knew that I once I did this, there was no turning back; and I was correct. After my first sexual experience, I knew it was wrong and yet I felt a sense of what I can only describe as satisfaction of some sort. I felt like I had finally accomplished what I had always wanted, which was positive attention from the opposite sex. Since my biological father wasn't paying me any attention at that time, I accepted this new relationship as its replacement.

Many months passed by, and I continued to sneak out the house at night or even would sneak him in my house just to have sex with the guy who I believed loved me. I found myself lying and being defensive all the time in attempts to keep others away because I felt like if anyone found out, he would be snatched out my life. I thought that this relationship was exactly what I had been missing my whole life. It was filled with lots of laughs, fun, joy, lots of attention which I always desired. Most importantly for me, it was a constant reminder that *I* was the one he wanted. Everything was all good until one day in the fall semester of my eleventh-grade year. I missed my menstrual cycle. My then dreamy world came crashing down into a million pieces.

Oh my gosh, I'm pregnant, I thought. During this time, I hadn't prayed in months and wasn't even trying to do anything God's way. My sixteen-year-old self was crying with no idea what to do next. I felt completely lost and scared because I was in no way capable of having a baby. When I finally told my boyfriend that I was pregnant, he looked just as scared as I was.

"What is it that you want to do?" he asked. I had no idea, but I knew I couldn't have a baby.

I told him that I was going to get rid of the baby, but I didn't know how or what to do. He told me that he would take care of everything and he would let me know the details. Over the next few days, I was praying that one day my cycle would magically appear, which never happened.

As the weeks progressed, I began to feel somehow connected to the person growing in my body. This connection caused doubts about moving forward with the plan. However, I was not in any position to take care of anyone. I later found out that in my state, there were laws in place that prohibited young teenage girls from getting abortions without parental consent. I was devasted by that news. I knew that I could not tell my mother that I was pregnant—she would kill me! I had to figure out what to do. I ended up speaking to my aunt on my biological father's side of the family. She found a way around me telling my mother and helped me to get paperwork I needed. I encountered so many obstacles to just to get the paperwork that I almost gave up on it all. Eventually, I was able to speak with the people that made the decisions and ultimately moved forward.

That fall day, I stepped off the bus upon arrival at the clinic. As soon as my feet touched ground, I literally was sick to my stomach with fear. I feared getting rid of the baby growing inside of me, and I was scared about what they would do to me. Standing inside the clinic, I felt completely alone, as if no one else in the world felt as alone as I did. I checked in and waiting for the next steps. Eventually, my boyfriend showed up. We skipped school to do this.

As he sat next to me, he was completely silent. He didn't say anything more than asking me how I was feeling.

When my time came to go in the back of the clinic to be examined, I turned around and quickly glanced at my boyfriend sitting there. He gave me a semi smile before I walked through the doors.

Laying on the exam table in that small cold room, I wanted to cry and leave at that exact moment. The technician placed the probe on my stomach. She began to look for the baby and then I heard it. I heard the heartbeat of the person in my belly. I immediately began to cry.

"You're ten weeks pregnant. Did you know?" the technician asked. When she looked up at me, I was crying.

"You don't have to do this," she said before walking out of the room. She gave me a few minutes to make my final decision. I was overtaken by the emotions that were flooding my mind. I placed my hand on my stomach and cried even more. At that moment, I made the choice to terminate the pregnancy. I began to pray to God, asking Him to be with me. As I went through the procedure, I cried silently, realizing that I had murdered my own seed. The physical pain that I felt was nothing compared to the pain that I felt in my mind, emotions and spirit.

When the procedure was done, I was released to leave and follow up at the appointment given. As I walked out of the clinic I knew something had broken in me and I left a piece of me in that place. I went to my boyfriend's friend house to sleep a bit and recover because I couldn't go home early because I was skipping school.

Resting on his friend's couch, I felt horribly disgusted with myself. Over time, my physical body healed although my emotional self was broken. I no longer felt a need to be connected to anything that mattered. I continued to date my boyfriend, skip school and all types of mess. I started having dreams that tormented me about what I had done. I couldn't even pray. I heard a voice telling me that God no longer loved me because of the choice I made. I heard that voice so often that I believed it. My relationship with God completely took a backseat because I could not stand myself so how would God even still love me knowing that I killed my baby.

I want you to know that God never runs away from us. God is not afraid or intimidated by our mistakes or choices. He desires us to run to Him because He is our safe place. He wants to heal our wounds and insecurities. At the time of the abortion, I didn't know these things about God; however, I eventually learned.

The name of the LORD is a strong tower;
The righteous runs to it and is safe and set on high [far above evil].
Proverbs 18:10 AMP

Over the next few months, I found myself in a whirlwind. I was trying to fill another hole, but this hole was one that I created. I decided to dig my feet in more in the relationship with my boyfriend. I desired him to be the only one who I would accept emotional support from. Although he attempted to fill this void, he himself was just as broken as I was at that time. He, too, came from a broken home. He thought that I would soothe his wounds with my love and attention and I looked for him to do the same for me. I continued to give my body, time, gifts, love and attention to him, believing that if I gave him all these things, he would fill my own voids.

I placed my expectation on him for my happiness. My seventeenth birthday came, and I was excited because my time dwelling in the dysfunction was almost up. My household only became more contentious and having peace in that home was a difficult thing to accomplish. Most of the time, my siblings and I would either stay in our rooms or we found other places to go. My parents continued to argue and fight, and I no longer desired to be there.

Being the oldest child in the house came with so many responsibilities and watching my siblings was one of the biggest things I did. One day, I was in charge while my parents were gone to work. I attempted to get my little sister to clean up as usual. This particular day, she refused to do anything.

Of course, because we are siblings, we argued and fought about it, but it got done.

When my parents came home, I was yet again called down to them and I was interrogated. My sister told my parents that I basically jumped on her. My stepfather was yet again upset and did not allow me to fully share my side of the story. So, we ended up arguing. The argument escalated as it had in the past. My mother stood there, yelling at us both before my stepfather walked up on me.

"Dominique, why do you keep doing this?" my mother asked. I looked at her and I felt completely abandoned—this time by the one who should've stood up for me. In that next moment, I told my stepfather to get out my face or else.

"What are you gonna do?" he responded before shoving me. I began fighting him like I was fighting someone in the streets. My mother broke up the fight and I felt enraged by everything and everyone. My mother called the police. When the police arrived, she made up another story which didn't include the truth. As I stood in the living room listening to the lie, I knew I had to get out of this situation. I was left with a busted lip, black eye and a bruised eye socket, and a mother who I did not know. I called my aunt who came and picked me up. I left that house with no intention of returning.

My mother's decision to remain in a relationship that was and had been toxic for so many years created this mindset that fighting was the only way to survive. After that situation, fighting became my new normal. I never wanted to feel vulnerable, which equaled weakness to me. I promised myself that I would not end up in a relationship like my mother's. I decided that for me to have a relationship different from one like my mother's, this is who I needed to become. I would always defend myself and my values to the death if need be because I declared that I would never take that level of disrespect ever.

After that altercation, my choices continued to be solely about how I felt and what I desired to do. I did not care about those who didn't care about me. I stayed with my aunt for a great portion of my senior year of high school. During the first few days there with my aunt, she would just let me cry and talk without judging me for my thoughts, anger or hurt. My aunt went to my mother's job where she did karaoke and got only one bag of my clothes. When my aunt returned home, I was completely shocked that only the few items placed in that bag was I had in the lonely world that I was living in.

Throughout my senior year, I was trying to figure out a way to never return to my parents' house. At this point, I no longer wanted to talk about my feelings about home life. Honestly, I had no desire to discuss my feelings, period. My aunt became the woman who I looked to when it came to showing and teaching me about entering the real world. My aunt was a strong, resilient woman who was yet soft, sweet and super feminine. She was a lioness and a warrior who protected those she loved by any means necessary. Over time, I began to see up close and personal all of these sides of her. This made me want to figure out how to overcome my horrible experiences.

My senior year continued with much progress. The senior pinning ceremony came and went, and my parents were not in attendance. The National Honor Society events came and still, no parents. The only ones who supported me at that time where my aunt and my boyfriend. Although I was moving forward in many areas of my life, I still felt rejected and abandoned. Not knowing what to do or who to turn to, I leaned more into my boyfriend. I continued to skip school and have sex, but I made sure I returned to school to be picked up. I was so careful to make sure that I kept up the appearances because I felt like my young heart couldn't handle anymore rejection.

After those few months, my aunt told me that I had to return to my parents' home. My aunt looked completely heartbroken and helpless. I was told that there were several conversations which ended in me having to go home. My heart felt like it was in my stomach; I was speechless. I knew that this was somehow an important moment in my life, but I had no idea what way it was going to come out for me.

When I returned home, it felt quite strange. I felt like I wasn't supposed to be there. The atmosphere definitely felt different as well. My mother was excited to have me home, along with my siblings. I didn't see my stepfather initially. When I did see him, he gave the good ole "what's up" and kept it moving. I decided to stay out of the way as much as possible, and this strategy worked for me.

My mother allowed me to do things that teenagers should do like hang with friends and take driver's training classes. The fact that I would ask her for things, and it was a non-delayed yes actually made me leery. I figured that all of her "yes" responses were her apologies for all the crap that happened. One day, I came home from school and there was a gold Ford Tempo in front of our house. I asked who was visiting us and the response I received was one I wasn't prepared to hear.

"That is your car."

To my amazement, I was rendered speechless. I instantly felt a bit of freedom which I took full advantage of at that time. I drove myself to school, my friend's house and of course, I skipped my afternoon classes to be with my boyfriend. Even though I knew that my decisions were horrible for my future, I didn't care because at least I was making these decisions and not being subjected to other people's.

Springtime rolled around and I was living my best life. It was no turning back from there. Then I began to feel sick in the mornings before school every day. Initially, I didn't think anything of it until I realized that I'd missed my menstrual cycle. Honestly, I didn't panic or become fearful; I just knew that I was pregnant. So, I decided to find out for sure. When the clinic confirmed the pregnancy, I sat in the exam room contemplating how I was going to tell my parents and raise my child. I left that clinic, totally clueless as to the next steps to take, but I knew that I had to do something.

When I got home, I sat in my room and I called my boyfriend and told him that I needed to see him. He came shortly thereafter and when I told him that I was pregnant and that I was going to keep this baby, he gave me all sorts of reasons about why we should and why we shouldn't, but he told me that the decision was ultimately up to me. We sat in his car, talking about what our future will look like. Neither one of us had any idea about what to do. We both knew that we did not want our child to grow up in the way that we did. So we made a vow to make sure that never happened.

A few days after I found out that I was pregnant, my mom called me down from my room. When I got to the bottom of the stairs, she was holding a pregnancy test. She told me that she noticed that I didn't have a cycle and she wanted to see if I was pregnant. I looked my mother directly in her eyes and told her I didn't need to take a pregnancy test.

"Why not?" she asked. I told her that I knew that I was pregnant, that I was going to have a baby and that we would have insurance.

My mother told me that she wanted me to take the test anyway, and I firmly told her no. In that moment, I felt proud of myself. Honestly, I do not know why I felt proud. Maybe it was because I had stood up to the person who caused me so much heartache by the decisions that she had made over the course of my life.

Moments after I told my mom that I was pregnant, she told me how I needed to get rid of my baby and how that will be the best thing for me. She continued by saying that my life will be greater and better if I did not have this child. But my mother didn't know that I had already had an abortion. She didn't know that I could not live with the pain and heartache that having an abortion caused, and I dare not do it again. So of course, that new information caused a great ripple effect in my household and in my family. My mother got on the phone and called all my aunts. Their conversations revolved around what I should do, how they were so disappointed in me and how they just didn't understand why I would choose to have this baby.

Within hours of me telling my mother, my aunts were at the house. They told me how I was about to ruin my life and how I would never become anything more than a statistic. They told me that I would live in poverty and not experience life. My aunts told me how my boyfriend would leave me and never marry me. They told me all types of things that I guess they believed would encourage me to get rid of my baby. As I sat there at times trying to defend my decision, I realized that I was completely alone. The only person I would be able to lean on would be my boyfriend and the God that I had not spoken to.

At the time, I didn't know that this "reality check" would be burned into mind for years, and that I would make decisions based upon the things these women said to me. I was determined to prove them wrong at any cost and unfortunately, I paid a great price. It wasn't long after the reveal of my pregnancy that I graduated high school and I found myself making a life-changing decision.

My stepfather and mother came home drunk yet again, and fussing was the last thing I wanted to hear. I found myself being asked again about the way I managed things while they were gone. I let their aggressive words and tone slide because I was accustomed to this behavior at this point. As I sat there listening, my stepfather increased his tone and pushed the dining room table into my stomach. I quickly reminded him that I was pregnant and asked that he remember that. My comment obviously did not mean anything because he continued to push the table, so much so that I rose up from the table.

As I walked away, my stepfather stood up and blocked me from leaving. I told him that I was not going to fight him, and someone would be leaving in body bag that night. He stood there in shock. I looked at my mother and I said, "Mama, it's either him or me. You choose." The look in my mother's eyes was heartbreaking because I knew I was not her choice.

"Dominique, why are you doing this? You need to stop it." I looked my mother in the eyes and I said, "No need to choose, Mama. I am going to leave." I took my seventeen-year-old self to my room, packed everything I could fit in my backpack, grabbed a jacket and proceeded to leave. I came back downstairs and headed towards the front door. In my heart, I wanted to hear my mom say wait, but it never happened. She stood there in her drunkenness, and said, "If you leave, do not come back." That's when I walked out that house and I didn't look back.

As I walked down the street in the middle of the night, crying uncontrollably. I found a payphone and I called my boyfriend crying, trying to explain what happened. I ended up standing at the bus stop until he came to pick me up. He took me to his grandmother's house where he lived because he left his parents' house due to his father beating him. I cried that whole night, feeling completely broken in every way. I had no way to fix it and I was about to become someone's mother. All I knew in that moment was hurt and pain. Although I hadn't spoken to God, I had to believe that He was near and would not let me die in my devastation.

The LORD is near to the heartbroken
And He saves those who are crushed in spirit (contrite in heart, truly sorry for their sin). Many hardships and perplexing circumstances confront the righteous,
But the LORD rescues him from them all.
Psalms 34:18-19 AMP

I want you to be healed from the decisions of your past and the decisions of others. I want you to be made free by the truth that God already knew what you would do, experience, overcome and become even at this very moment. God even knew that at this exact moment, you would be reading a book that speaks to the deepest parts of your soul.

I can look back on this place in my life and see how much I was hurting myself. It explains why I allowed so many cycles of dysfunction to occur for years. Please understand how the decisions of others can greatly affect how you look at people, situations, the choices before you and your view of yourself. Notice how I made decisions out of my trauma, rejections, and abandonment and how I didn't even view my own self as valuable at all. The stings I felt from the wrong choices I made were easier to deal with than the constant rejection by the people around me. Although I know many of the choices I made caused me some level of pain—compromise, low self-esteem and feeling inadequate, I sacrificed myself to feel like I belonged even for a moment. I continually was looking for others to validate me, my feelings and even my identity, only to be left feeling emptier than when I started. This mindset unfortunately translated over in every relationship I had.

How many times have you allowed the decisions of others hold you hostage? How many times have you sacrificed yourself just to belong? For years, I allowed other people's choices to hold me hostage because of how I felt. Not recognizing that I allowed the choices of others keep me in a place of perpetual rejection and people pleasing. I allowed rejection and abandonment to make decisions for me because it was all I've known. I allowed rejection and abandonment tell me what I should expect, how I was to be treated, how I should view myself and how I should give and receive attention and love.

Remember the enemies of your destiny and purpose desire for you to have what is known as "arrested development," which means that you emotionally and mentally stop growing due to the trauma you experienced. You may ask, who are the destiny enemies? The answer is simple: your trauma, hurt, pain, rejection, molestation, sexual experiences, your childhood and every other place that floods your mind, brings tears to your eyes and pain to the surface. So many men and women are aging in years but are stuck at the age where they experienced trauma.

In this very moment, I want you to think about the situations that caused you to make certain decisions or even become a version of yourself that you never even thought you would be. Ask yourself this question: Am I arrested developmentally in my emotions and mindset? If your answer is yes—as mine was, I want you to know that God has and is the solution. The solution is the uncovering of your identity that comes from Him. God does not desire for us to live hostage to anything. He isn't surprised by the choices you've made or the choices of others for you. Your mistakes, poor choices, hurt, neglect, abuse, depression and every other destructive thing isn't too much for Him to handle. God desires us to be free from every place of bondage.

But now, this is what the LORD, your Creator says, O Jacob,
And He who formed you, O Israel,
"Do not fear, for I have redeemed you [from captivity];
I have called you by name; you are Mine!
When you pass through the waters, I will be with you;
And through the rivers, they will not overwhelm you.
When you walk through fire, you will not be scorched,
Nor will the flame burn you.
Isaiah 43:1-2 AMP

The Bible says that God is concerned about the things that concern us. If you are reading this, then you have a desire to be made whole in some area of your life.

God is concerned about that and will complete it until the end.

I am convinced and confident of this very thing, that He who has begun a good work in you will [continue to] perfect and complete it until the day of Christ Jesus [the time of His return].

Philippians 1:6 AMP

The beautiful thing that I love about God is that although the enemies of our lives come to distract, derail and destroy us, God does not want us to stay in that place. By His spirit, He will by any means necessary get a message to you to let you know that He's still there. God sees just where you've been and where you're going. It's never too late to come to the Father and ask to be healed from the pain of your history.

Pray this prayer:

Heavenly Father, I thank you that your word says that I can come boldly to your throne, asking anything in Jesus' name and you are just to do it. Today, I bring my mustard seed of faith before you, knowing that you hear me as I pray. Father, my heart's desire is to be made whole today. I am reaching for the hem of your garment this day to be made whole from the place of my past decisions and even the decisions others made for me. Lord, I choose to forgive myself and those who helped create this empty space in my soul. Lord, I thank you that my past does not determine my future. I have determined in my heart and mind to trust you in my process of healing; with you, all things are possible.

Father, your word says that you are near to the brokenhearted and crushed in spirit. I give you full access to the darkest places of my heart. Mend me and restore me, Father. I thank you that the wounds of my past will no longer lead me, but I will be led by the spirit of life and truth that is only found in you.

Lord, I thank you that I have chosen to walk with you and be the willing vessel to crush the plans of the enemy against me and the generations that will come from me. I will yield to your voice and be made whole. Have your way *in my mind, body and soul. Renew your spirit in me so that I may fulfill my purpose and destiny. Lord, I love you and thank you for loving me through it all. Amen.*

Though I walk in the midst of trouble, You will revive me; You will stretch out Your hand against the wrath of my enemies,

And Your right hand will save me.

The LORD will accomplish that which concerns me;

Your [unwavering] lovingkindness, O LORD, endures forever—

Do not abandon the works of Your own hands.

Psalm 138:7-8 AMP

Chapter Five: Rejected and Married

For most people, the word "marriage" produces feelings of love, safety, security, loyalty and commitment, amongst other things. I am inclined to believe that many little girls and boys dream of their wedding day, where they put on their wedding attire and marry the mate of their dreams. That was even my dream when I was a little girl. I remember playing with my Barbie dolls with my cousins, and we would always pretend that I would get married. Even as I entered my journey as a young adult, marriage was still something that I desired.

I believed that once I got married, the holes from the pains of my past would disappear. I believed that I would be with the man who would fill the holes with his love and presence. I didn't have any idea of the great weight or responsibility that marriage carried. I thought that love was all I would need. It's so important that every man and woman reading this be ready to look at the decisions you've made from the beginning up to this point. Dismiss any thoughts of your trauma and dysfunction not playing a part in the person you are now or the things that you've accepted and expected especially in your relationships.

I was seventeen years old, eight months pregnant living in my boyfriend's parents' house after I decided to leave my own home. I felt so uncomfortable living in that home because I needed my own place to build my own family. I remember a conversation that was my first indication that I was in the wrong relationship. I spoke to my boyfriend one day about moving once the baby came and how we should start our own family in our new home. He looked at me dead in my eyes and said, "Dominique, I will never get married because I do not see the point. So, I hope you're not looking for that in the future." Sitting in the little work room where we were, I looked at him and said a simple "okay."

I got up, feeling crushed again because I thought that he loved me enough to one day consider marriage, but nope; it was not for him. I never thought he would have said that to me, considering all the things we had endured up to that point. Soon after, our son was born, and everything seemed to be okay for a while. Our relationship went through so many changes. I moved out of his parents' house and got an apartment. We started having arguments about all of his female "friends" and how they called him all the time. We argued about how he would yell and scream at me about the simplest things. Here I am, not understanding my own value, I would continue to try to talk him down and just comply with whatever would make him happy. I wanted him to love me, be nice and to accept me.

Over time, things between us continued to be rocky, up and down all the time. The arguments worsened and was often accentuated with screaming and hollering. He started to lie all the time about being places and ultimately, I found out that there were other women in the picture. I endured the cheating, lying and disrespect on every level until I was twenty years old. That's when I recognized that either something was absolutely wrong with me or him. I called it quits and decided to work on myself figuring out me.

Although I called it quits, I still continued to be intimate with my ex-boyfriend because it was what I knew to do, and it was convenient. How many of us have fallen prey to this notion? Although I knew at that time that he wasn't good for me, I felt like maybe he would begin to really see me considering I was still willing to sleep with him. I found myself praying that he would grow up and I would be better for him.

The Bible says in 1 Corinthians 6:19 that our bodies are temples of the Holy Spirit. This means that we should respect the presence of God within us. I had no idea that sharing my body continuously with a toxic spirit would continue to break and weaken me emotionally, mentally and spiritually to the point that anything would go.

A year later, I had reached a place where I had been consistently working on my relationship with God. I knew that I had some issues, but I didn't know the depth of my trauma. I would often pray, asking God to somehow mend the holes that I felt, but nothing changed. God promises us that He won't leave or forsake us ever, but I want you to know that until you go back to those places and situations, and deal with the people who caused your trauma, you will remain broken just like I was. God will not force you, but He will be ready when you decide.

While I was not with my ex-boyfriend, during that time he seemed to be "maturing." During our conversations, it seemed as if he was thinking about his future. He was more at peace and was even treating me completely different. He expressed his desire to be with me and to grow a family with me.

He told me how much he needed me and that he would spend more time with me. He would complement me and tell me I was the most beautiful thing he ever saw. I eventually gave into his many words, we had sex and I became pregnant with our second child.

Not many days after I found out, I told him that I was pregnant.

"Well, it ain't my baby. We only have had sex that one time," he responded rather quickly. I was completely floored and confused because of all the things he had been saying to me for months before I gave into him. I went back home to my apartment and cried my eyes out. I didn't understand how and why he continued to reject me. I cried out to God on my living room floor, begging Him to remove everything in me that made me even desire my ex. In that moment, I asked God to take full control of my life because I had made so many mistakes after giving my life to Him at age thirteen, and I was tired of hurting. When I got up off my floor that night, I rose up still feeling hurt and rejected; however, I knew God heard me. I did not know how or when I would begin to heal, but I trusted God.

It took months for me to even speak to my ex after sharing the news of my pregnancy. I loved him but I never understood why I felt compelled to figure things out, no matter how long I stopped speaking or stopped seeing him.

While my pregnancy continued to progress, I moved into a new home and was doing well. My ex eventually came to me and apologized about saying the baby wasn't his and he wanted to start a new path in his life. He told me he was going to be truck driving to make more money and have time alone with God. I verbalized to him that I hope he found a closer relationship with God and whatever else he desired, but we wouldn't be getting back to together.

After he left the state to drive across country, I gave birth to our second son. Although we were not in a relationship, he would call me while he drove across the country, telling me about the things he saw and the conversations he had with God and how he would answer so many of his questions. I thought that was great and even attractive that he desired to know more about the things of God. But see, the problem here that I now can recognize is that although he was talking with God and he was receiving a response, my ex wasn't allowing God to heal his hurt, broken and dysfunctional places. He was only interested in conversations but not transformation.

We continued to have these in-depth conversations about what we desired to do and become in our individual relationships with God. He would call me and tell me that he was foolish for how he treated me in years past and that he was done acting immature. His speech was so consistent that I went from blowing him off completely to actually believing him. Then the day came that he purposed in his heart to ask me to marry him during a phone conversation while he was driving in another state.

When he asked me to marry him, my immediate response was no. Now looking back, I now know that was my spirit warning me not to proceed. I told him that he wasn't serious about me and that I was just his comfort zone—which I also now know was the absolute truth. He told me he was going to show me how serious he really was. He eventually showed up in Michigan and proposed to me again, saying all the things a young woman who has two children by her teenage love would dream to hear. At that moment, I stood there with him as he awaited my answer. Meanwhile, I was at war with myself on the inside. I felt like wow, this moment is all I have thought about for most of my adult life. He picked me after everyone told me he never would marry me—and even after he vowed he would *never* marry. Then, the other side of me remembered all the hurt and pain, and how hard I had worked to get over it, not ever expecting him to really change. In that moment, I chose not to go with the gut feeling to maintain my no, but I decided to marry him to prove everyone else wrong. He had picked me, and our love would heal each other and the world, so I said *yes!*

If you do not remember anything else from reading this book, highlight this.

Any relationship that has a foundation built upon each other's mutual pain, dysfunction, trauma, rejection and abandonment will *never* work. Why? Because you will forever find yourself pouring everything you have and are into a cup with a hole in the bottom. You will never be enough for that person, ever.

If you desire a relationship to last the test of time, it needs to be built on the solid rock, whose name is Jesus Christ.

"So everyone who hears these words of Mine and acts on them, will be like a wise man [a far-sighted, practical, and sensible man] who built his house on the rock. And the rain fell, and the floods and torrents came, and the winds blew and slammed against that house; yet it did not fall, because it had been founded on the rock. And everyone who hears these words of Mine and does not do them, will be like a foolish (stupid) man who built his house on the sand. And the rain fell, and the floods and torrents came, and the winds blew and slammed against that house; and it fell—and great and complete was its fall."

Matthew 7:24-27 AMP

Just like any other twenty-three-year-old woman who was recently proposed to, I was excited about the new life that I would have as a wife and mother. I was excited to begin my journey to create new family traditions and to ultimately raise my children in a household that would be drama free. Our wedding was planned in eight months after he proposed. During that time, many of my family members came to me, asking me if I was certain that this what I really wanted. I told them that I was ready to marry my high school sweetheart. Deep inside my heart, I had doubts; however, I was committed to my decision.

The day before I got married, my mother asked me if I was certain that I wanted to marry my future husband. I remember it as if it happened yesterday.

"Dominique, are you sure that you want to do this? You can save this dress and we can just have a family party instead of a reception. I don't think this is going to be right."

"Yes, Mama I'm ready and I'm sure that I want to marry him," I responded. My mother never asked me again after that moment.

My wedding day came and went with the blink of eye and our marital covenant began. I was so happy to be married; I felt like the happiest woman ever. But my beautiful, wedded bliss would quickly be turned into a living hell.

We got married in July; when January came, my world was crushed. My cousin died from complications of lupus that January. This cousin and I were born thirty days apart and we were close like sisters. I was completely devastated, and I expected my new husband to be by my side comforting and supporting me. Unfortunately, I went through this deep grief all alone. I remember sitting on the end of my bed, crying and feeling completely alone. I knew that I had to be there for my family and pay my respects to my cousin; otherwise, I would never forgive myself.

Up until that moment, my husband had been so mellow and the few disagreements we had were easy to overcome. I remember having a conversation with my husband, explaining my devastation. The look on his face was flat void of emotion and his response was callous. At that moment, I knew that this was probably the beginning of more hurt and callous behavior. I told him that I was going to be with my family and help with the arrangements. He responded by saying that he didn't want me to attend because he had to work. I was absolutely devastated! The man who I married six months ago looked me in the face and crushed me with his words. Sad to say, it was the first time but definitely not the last.

Later that week, I traveled to be with my family as planned and left him with the kids. Never in a million years would I have thought I could feel so alone in a relationship with the person who I just vowed to spend my life with. While I was grieving with my family, I thought that would be the most hurt I could endure at that moment, but I was wrong. Sitting on the tub, I was on the phone listening to my husband screaming at me because he was mad that I had left him at home to take the kids to school. I felt like the dumbest person in the world because all the changes that I saw in my husband before we got married had been false. I saw the side of the person that I thought was gone.

I sat there crying and brokenhearted twice over because of the death of my cousin and the fact that I stood before God and vowed to be in covenant with a man who *I knew* had not changed. My soul was devastated because the vows I took meant so much to me and I would have to figure out how to make my marriage successful.

I want you to remember something when it comes to relationships of any kind. What you see with your eyes and know in your spirit about someone usually is the truth. If I had not been broken, insecure and rejected, I would have never married that man or endured as much hell. As the time concluded with my family, I knew that I had to return home to a man who I was completely hurt by and return to being his wife and a mother to our children.

When I returned home, I stayed quiet for a while because although I was hurting, I was too scared to speak up. What if I made him upset and he left? I know that sounds backwards. It's like, *so what if he's mad and leaves? He just devastated you and he did not even care.* But that's not how a rejected mind and spirit works. The goal is the keep them around because unfortunately, they temporarily fill that hole on the inside and the hurt, pain, rejection are just results of the choice.

As time went on, the dysfunction went on as well. When you do not understand your identity and purpose in

Christ, anything goes, and you learn to bear it. That's what was happening with me. I began to bear the weight of the relationship solely by myself. All the things that I had told myself I would not tolerate became my reality. I did what any other broken person does:

I buried it. I buried the pain, hurt, disappointment, embarrassment, abuse, neglect under fake smiles that used to be real. When you're broken, it is easier to hide and bury things than it is to face them head on. When you do decide to confront the issues, you approach them from the place of your rejection, which changes nothing.

I continued to deal with the rollercoaster that I would call my marriage. The issues in my marriage continued to grow more difficult over time.

I found myself losing more of the person who I knew was down on the inside. So many nights were spent arguing and screaming with my husband, trying to get him to hear me and see me. I had learned to behave like him, with all the yelling and screaming, thinking that it had to break something in him to see the woman standing in front of him begging to be loved differently.

As the years went by, I found myself going through cycles of depression. I begged him to go to counseling to save our marriage and he always responded by saying that he didn't need anyone to tell him anything. I began to sink to what I believed was the bottom, but this hole felt bottomless. Eventually, I found out that my husband was cheating on me for long periods of time with women in other states while he worked.

After giving birth to our third son, a woman called his phone. I picked up the phone thinking it was his job, only to hear a female's voice on the other end. I stood there frozen in my kitchen as this woman asked to speak to my husband. I asked her who she was, and she responded. I asked her if she had slept with my husband and her answered cause my knees to buckle underneath me.

"Not this time; I didn't feel like driving to his hotel," she replied. I thanked her for the information and hung up the phone. I stood in my kitchen confused and shocked, looking at my newborn son who was asleep in his bouncer seat. I fell to my knees, crying uncontrollably because I thought that all the things I had done showed him how much I loved him. I thought that me accepting his repeated apologies for all his wrong deeds proved my love for him. I just knew that eventually he would have outgrown these horrible stages of life. I believed what I heard from other women when they said all men go through growing pains and to just deal with it because he will eventually see that you are the one for him. Let me dispel a lie right now. Your strength is determined by how much pain and hurt you can endure from someone. Your strength is determined by how quickly you discover your identity in Christ and release people and situations that cause your repeated trauma.

Despite going through all sorts of hell, I was overwhelmed with my desire to make this marriage work that all the standards I had disappeared. At this juncture, I no longer even knew what the standard should even be. Everything inside of me was screaming and I did not know how to fix it. I knew that I had to return to my first love, who is my heavenly Father. I knew that my relationship with God needed to be priority.

Although I had been praying and reading my Word, I needed to do something different to get a new result. I determined in my heart to surrender my marriage to God and allow Him to fix it. Somewhere in my heart, I believed that God would fix it, even though I had not even invited Him into the marriage from the beginning.

During the first few years of my marriage, I did things the way that I knew how. I didn't understand the purpose of marriage or God's heart in marriage. I eventually got water baptized for the second time during those first few years, and I was baptized by the Holy Spirit, which forever changed my life. Some may not understand the importance of these pivotal moments but let me explain it to you. The enemies of rejection, trauma, abuse, neglect and the other sorts watch and study you. They are the decision makers for you, as I discussed previously. When the Spirit of God is upon you and then lives inside of you, things are going to change forever. "Why?" you may ask? Because the Spirit of God teaches you all things. The ways, responses, reactions, conversations you had previously completely change because your purpose and destiny fills your life more than the trash of your past.

After being filled with the spirit of God and my husband knowing this, I felt like it would grow us closer because he would know for sure that God was leading me, but not so. My marriage continued to go through cycles of horrible treatment and repeated apologies. My husband would even muster up tears at times, explaining to me that he never learned how to love and that he needed me to continue to teach him. He told me that he was going to change and grow to become better. His behavior would change for a few weeks—sometimes months at a time, but then return to the same old mess.

I went through some major depression, trying to wrap my mind around the way to fix the marriage. That's when I heard the voice of God say, "Let me fix you." I knew clearly that I needed the fixing. As I continued to let God heal me, I began to move more towards my purpose. I started singing on the praise team at church, attended

Bible study and I made my prayer time a priority. As I began to do these things, my husband's actions worsened. Please understand that the Bible says we do not fight flesh and blood, but we battle with spirits (Ephesians 6:12). So, the spirit in my husband at that time was enraged that the old tactics to make me argue and fight had changed. I no longer desired to do those things anymore because I would go pray. The more that you begin to heal and discover your identity, purpose and destiny, the more hell throws at you.

For our struggle is not against flesh and blood [contending only with physical opponents], but against the rulers, against the powers, against the world forces of this [present] darkness, against the spiritual forces of wickedness in the heavenly (supernatural) places.
Ephesians 6:12 AMP

The more I moved towards the things of God, the more that I understood that it was not my responsibility to make my husband whole. Over time, I understood that my wholeness and identity was not founded in my husband. I realized that I was put here in the earth to be more than just a mother and wife. I had a kingdom mandate.

As I continued to grow closer to my Father in heaven, the more I changed. As I began to change, God began to tell me who I was and what I deserved, just like an awesome father should. But simultaneously, my relationship continued to spiral downward so much so that we would not speak for days—even weeks on end. Whenever we did have a conversation, it would end in an argument. The arguments continued to escalate over time. When we were out in public or around family, my husband would cater to me and act as if we had the greatest relationship ever. But privately, he became physically abusive. He began pushing me into corners, smacking my face and he even choking me at times. But then he would later come back to me and express how sorry he was.

I was beginning to understand what I deserved, however the enemy always reminded me about the covenant that I made. I felt like if I let go of the marriage, I was failing God.

I just knew that as a wife, it was my job to forgive him; but I did not comprehend that I was harming myself and showing my children that dysfunction was normal. I knew that the actions in my marriage were wrong and I desired God to fix it. I would often pray that God would fix my husband, to mend him and heal him. Other times, I prayed for God to whoop him because of all the pain he was causing me.

In all the times I would pray these prayers, God did not speak with me about him; God would only show me *myself and my trauma*. God told me to give Him the things

He showed me. Since my heart desired Him and to be more like Him, I would quickly hand those things right over to God. Just as fast as God shows you your trauma and you give those things to Him, He is just to heal you. Surrendering your heart to God draws Him closer to you. He will touch the place of your infirmity in an instant.

I am sure that my story regarding my marriage isn't something that you've never heard before; unfortunately, occurrences like this are probably quite common. In my marriage of eleven years, I've experienced more heartache than happiness. I endured the lies, cheating, abuse, and neglect. I've cried many tears, experienced pain, sorrow, heartbreak and humiliation too many times to count. But in the glimpses of happiness during the relationship, I saw the potential of the man my husband could be with Christ, which remained in the forefront of my mind. The potential I saw became my strands of hope for my marriage during the difficult times.

As I continued to mature in my relationship with God, things only became even more toxic. I felt the increased tension and weight of the marriage, my children's hearts if I choose to leave, and the criticism of others. It was all too heavy. I never wanted to be the reason that my marriage and family failed. All I wanted was the family and marriage that I had dreamed about the majority of my life. But the more that I pursued my destiny, the stronger the attacks became from the obvious opposing spirit in my husband.

There were times where my husband would start arguments with me every Sunday morning just so that I could be late to service and unable to serve. He would yell at me saying that "the church" was more important than my family. He told me that I needed to stop singing and attending church every week and work on my relationship with him. After having this conversation with him, I went to my bedroom and cried because I felt like I had to make a choice. I thought that maybe if I stop attending church, maybe things would get better in my relationship with my husband, and he would return to church with me. So, I decided to stop attending for a season and work diligently on my marriage.

If you had not guessed, the peace in my home only lasted for a moment because even after I made the choice to stop attending church, I realized it was never about me serving or attending church. It was a tactic of manipulation and control to halt me from forward movement towards my destiny. I learned very quickly after this situation that relationships in my life should push me closer to Christ, not drag me away from Him. All hell broke loose in my life and household, and yet I still held on to the strands of potential in my husband because otherwise, I would have to tell him that the marriage was truly over.

Sometimes, it is easier to tell yourself that you're doing the right thing by staying in a toxic relationship because you want to spare the other person's feelings, but in reality, you're really hurting yourself. I had my pastor and my friends praying, and I began to fast and pray all the time in an attempt for something different to happen in my marriage. Even though the relationship was rough, I just knew that God was going to move on my behalf because I was being obedient and was doing all the things that I knew were right before God. But the thing that I did not give much consideration to,
was my husband's *free will.*

I, of course, had thought about him not ever really changing, but I thought that because we were married, it could happen for us one day because he told me he loved me. The unsanctified husband could be saved by me showing a Christ-filled life.
I had been considering filing for divorce for months towards the end of the relationship because I could no longer allow myself and my children to experience this level of dysfunction. I so desired to be in a whole relationship with a man who had Christ at the center of his life. Deep down in my heart, I knew that the way my husband saw me was

completely unhealthy and that he didn't know me or my heart.

Several days before I was certain the marriage was over, my husband flipped out and kidnapped our children. He refused to tell me where any of them were. The dread and heartbreak I felt not knowing if he was going to return home with them was horrible. When my son called me and told me that he and his siblings were home after ten plus hours of being gone, I was completely relieved. I had been driving all over the city, going to every place I thought they could be.

The moment I saw my children, I smiled at them, hugged them and went to my room and cried in my pillow. I prayed that day and asked God to give me the strength to leave but if I couldn't, then remove him from my life. I trusted God to do just what I asked.

Several days later, I stood outside a car dealership looking to purchase a car when my phone rang. It was a detective on the other end of the call. During the conversation, the detective began questioning me about me stealing guns and being accused of trying to kill my husband. I knew for sure at that moment that my husband never loved me, and our marriage was completely over.

As I explained the situation to the detective, I could not help but be in complete shock at the level of intentional hate coming from him. After our phone conversation, the detective told me he was going to close the case and that he was glad that I was getting out of that relationship. I filed for divorce within that week.

I've had time to look back over the course of the marriage, and I see the many places that the words and deeds didn't line up. Clearly, he didn't love me at all. His broken places loved the idea of me, but he didn't love the total me. The potential of a person and the reality of a person are two, completely different individuals. The only difference between the two is the person's willingness to move from potential to reality through their actions. Do not be the person who invests so much time into the potential of a person and never see that person become the reality because they were too broken to even see themselves.

Love endures with patience and serenity, love is kind and thoughtful, and is not jealous or envious; love does not brag and is not proud or arrogant. It is not rude; it is not self-seeking, it is not provoked [nor overly sensitive and easily angered]; it does not take into account a wrong endured. It does not rejoice at injustice, but rejoices with the truth [when right and truth prevail]. Love bears all things [regardless of what comes], believes all things [looking for the best in each one], hopes all things [remaining steadfast during difficult times], endures all things [without weakening].

1 Corinthians 13:4-7 AMP

Although I've experienced so much trauma during my marriage, I also gained so much insight and revelation of God and myself. The Bible is true when it talks about how God never leaves us or forsakes us in the good and bad times. During the hardest times in my marriage, I found myself crying out to God more. I found out that as I drew closer to Him, He came closer to me. I cultivated a relationship in prayer with God that I do not believe I could have gotten any other way. God always spoke to me about *me* and how He desired for me to grow. He did not even speak to me often concerning my husband. I later gained understanding that I was the only one in the marriage truly desiring to be made new from the inside out. I desired for God to heal the marriage even when I knew in my heart that it was in trouble. God always told me about who I was and the things that He called me to do.

Even though I had a natural father and stepfather, I never saw a healthy marital relationship which caused me to be ignorant of how to value myself and how to know what I deserve from the man I chose to be with. So, God, being an amazing heavenly Father, taught me my value and how I should be loved. I learned that I married out of my brokenness and rejection, but I had to allow God to heal the wounds of my past, which ultimately gave me the strength to leave a toxic relationship that was not bearing any fruit.

The Bible talks about knowing a tree by the fruit that it bears. You are probably thinking, what does that have to do with this? Your marriage should be a tree, rooted in a strong foundation which is found in Christ. It should be watered by the living water which is the Holy Spirit and producing fruit that people can see, can eat and be nourished by and not get sick from. It took me many years to get to the place that I accepted that my relationship and marriage was rooted incorrectly, and it was dead.

God never intended for our relationships to become the reason we are stagnant in life, never moving forward towards the things he placed us in the earth to accomplish. God created relationships to help us to flourish, grow, mature, die to our own ideas of ourselves and people, to learn to forgive and love in a Christ-centered way. Relationships are currency in the kingdom of God. They provide doors of opportunity, kingdom building, godly friendship and so much more. Therefore, it is vitally important for us to be healed, whole and to understand who we are so that we do not spend time waiting for a dead relationship to produce.

My heart's desire is that the experiences of my life and marriage will help you see the things, people and situations that have contributed to the decisions you have made over the course of your life. Although my marriage ended horribly, I am thankful for the journey because it made me the woman that I am today. So, if you're in a marriage or relationship now that looks or sounds similar to what you've read, know that God is able to fix it with two, willing surrendered people. Rejection does not have the last say about your relationships or your future. God's heart for you is to be made whole and become the tree with strong roots in Him. Pray this prayer:

Heavenly Father, I thank you for your lovingkindness towards me because it draws me to you. Lord, I ask that you show yourself mighty in this moment and forever more. I welcome you into every area of my life. I thank you that you are that yoke destroyer. Rejection, abandonment, fear, terror, hurt, pain, sorrow and every other spirit that does not produce your life-giving spirit is broken out of my life forever. I ask that you show and teach me my value through your word. I choose your plan, desires and purposes for my life that I may be a tree that produces much fruit. My desire is to become more like you daily, so I welcome your healing, your love and your thoughts about me. Lord, I thank you that you never will leave me or forsake me. I trust you with my life. In Jesus' Name. Amen.

And he will be like a tree firmly planted [and fed] by streams of water,
Which yields its fruit in its season;
Its leaf does not wither;
And in whatever he does, he prospers [and comes to maturity].
Psalm 1:3 AMP

Blessed [with spiritual security] is the man who believes and trusts in and relies on the LORD
And whose hope and confident expectation is the Lord.
For he will be [nourished] like a tree planted by the waters,
That spreads out its roots by the river;
And will not fear the heat when it comes;
But its leaves will be green and moist.
And it will not be anxious and concerned in a year of drought
Nor stop bearing fruit.
Jeremiah 17:7-8 AMP

Chapter Six: Forgiveness

The word *forgiveness* is a word that does not always produce feeling of joy.
Most times, this word has gotten a bad reputation, and in some circles it's like cursing. To forgive means to grant pardon to a person, to give up all claims on account. Knowing that the very definition of this word means to grant a pardon to someone is inconceivable to many of us because we have been hurt and damaged at the hands of another. But what if I told you that forgiveness was not about the other person, but about *you*?

I know that this may be a concept that sounds illogical but let me reassure you that it is true. After I filed for divorce after eleven years of marriage, I had lots of time to think about my marriage and the things that happened during that time. I felt many emotions during that timeframe, and it challenged every part of me to wrap my mind around forgiving him for all the pain he had caused me. Just when I thought he had done all that he could to hurt me during the marriage, I was wrong.

One fall evening, I came to my home to find that my front door had been kicked in. All of my jewelry and family heirlooms were stolen along with paperwork that only my ex knew where it was located. I was floored because I knew exactly who had stolen these items and violated my sense of security. Shortly after, I had to meet my ex to pick up an item for my child. The meetup was full of tension and then my ex did the usual. He threatened me and yelled in my face. Before I knew it, he punched me so hard in the face I was unconscious. I woke up sitting up in my car.

I looked at my face in the mirror to see my lip was completely split in two and I was bleeding from the back of my head. In the moments sitting in the emergency room, I was so hurt and angry, my blood was probably boiling. For some people, forgiveness comes easy to them and it's not issue. But for me, after the events of my marriage and experiencing violent domestic abuse on this level, it was overwhelming for me to even think about.

I was completely confused and so angry about everything. I had done right by him as a wife, and I was a good mother to our children. How could he split my lip like this and then lie about the events? On top of that, I had to drink my meals from a straw for weeks!

I'm sure many of you have had situations that produced new levels of anger that you didn't know you had. It was not until I had a true encounter with my own ideas about forgiveness against what God says that I was even open to this principle. And yes, I was saved and filled with the Holy Spirit, but it was hard for me to forgive. It was not until I was honest with God about the years of hurt, pain and anger that He was able to give me what I needed to forgive His way. God told me that the forgiveness was for me to be able to move on with my life, free of the power that unforgiveness produces. He explained to me that my willingness to forgive would free me and allow the blessing to continue to flow in my life. It took me a short period of time to get my mind to the place that I was ready to let it all go. I had to remember that God forgives me all the time. If I do not forgive, then God will not forgive me (Mark 11:26). We all need forgiveness that comes from His grace and mercy.

I shared this portion of my journey with you to show you that even in the worst situations, God is always near and that choosing to forgive produces a new level of freedom, joy and peace in any situation. Forgiveness allows your heart and spirit to be in right standing with God, which is what you should desire. In the moment I chose to forgive my ex, a weight was lifted off me. I had a peace, knowing that God protected me, and the purpose of my life has not been fulfilled yet, so the plan of hell to kill me failed. I challenge you to think about people and situations in your life that have caused you to walk in unforgiveness. Make the choice to release them because you deserve the freedom of a clear heart and mind. Remember, forgiveness is not for them but for *you*. Choose to live free in Christ.

Let all bitterness and wrath and anger and clamor [perpetual animosity, resentment, strife, fault-finding] and slander be put away from you, along with every kind of malice [all spitefulness, verbal abuse, malevolence]. Be kind and helpful to one another, tender-hearted [compassionate, understanding], forgiving one another [readily and freely], just as God in Christ also forgave you.

Ephesians 4:31-32 AMP

For if you forgive others their trespasses [their reckless and willful sins], your heavenly Father will also forgive you. But if you do not forgive others [nurturing your hurt and anger with the result that it interferes with your relationship with God], then your Father will not forgive your trespasses.

Matthew 6:14-15 AMP

Salvation

In the beginning, God created us in His image and likeness, not only to create another beautiful creation but to have relationship with us. His desire was for us always to be one with Him; but because of sin, we were disconnected from Him spiritually. God never wanted us to suffer the penalty of death, but He desired for us to live with Him for an eternity.

Say this aloud:

Lord, I confess with my mouth that I am sinner. I believe in my heart that Jesus Christ is the Son of God. I believe that He was born, He died for my sins and was raised from the dead and sits at the right hand of the Father. Come into my heart and be the Lord of my life. Thank you for your grace. I am saved. Amen.

www.ingramcontent.com/pod-product-compliance
Ingram Content Group UK Ltd.
Pitfield, Milton Keynes, MK11 3LW, UK
UKHW041931190726
13854UKWH00004B/1541

9 781667 189109